Very Simple
ARABIC

INCORPORATING

**Simple Etiquette in
Arabia**

Very Simple
ARABIC

INCORPORATING

Simple Etiquette in Arabia

Written and illustrated
by

James Peters

STACEY INTERNATIONAL

VERY SIMPLE ARABIC
incorporating
SIMPLE ETIQUETTE IN ARABIA

© Stacey International & James Peters 1994

Filmset by
SX Composing Limited, Rayleigh, Essex, England
Printed and bound by Tien Wah Press, Singapore

British Cataloguing in Publication Data.
A catalogue record for this book is available from the
British Library.

ISBN 0 905743 71 7

Simple Etiquette in Arabia first
published 1977; reprinted 1979 & 1981

Very Simple Arabic first published 1980

Fully revised combined edition
first published 1994

Reprinted 1995, 1997, 2000

Stacey International
128 Kensington Church Street
London W8 4BH
Fax: (0)171 792 9288
E-mail: 106463.424@compuserve.com

Introduction

It is a well known fact that the smallest efforts of the foreigner in learning Arabic can earn a disproportionate amount of kudos and appreciation.

Speaking Arabic need not be difficult – even for those who claim to be bad at languages. *Very Simple Arabic* is a highly selective phrase-book and elementary language guide. The few vital phrases needed in the most commonly experienced situations can be quickly found. For those who wish to go further I have also included a simple explanation of grammar and a vocabulary of useful words.

Etiquette is important in Arabia. Indeed, you must know something about it if you wish to get on well with Arabs. But it does take time to pick up – time you may not have.

In *Simple Etiquette in Arabia*, I have tried to provide the key common denominators of etiquette pertaining to this vast area, yet keeping a particular eye on those countries which could be broadly classed as 'The Gulf Region'. For the businessman this is undoubtedly one of the most active areas in the whole of Arabia.

JAMES PETERS

A Note on Pronunciation

Arabic words in the text are intended to be pronounced exactly as the English spelling suggests. There are some sounds, however, which are not found in English and these are given below:

aa	*is pronounced as*	'a' in 'father'
ow	,,	,,	'ow' in 'how'
u	,,	,,	'u' in 'put'
dh	,,	,,	'th' in 'the'
kh	,,	,,	'ch' in 'loch'
gh	,,	,,	'r' in French 'rue'
ai	,,	,,	'eye'
q	,,	,,	guttural 'k'
'	,,	,,	glottal stop

Where necessary the stress syllable is underlined. Doubled consonants are given extra stress. Finally, the definite article 'al' is linked to its noun or adjective by a hyphen.

Acknowledgements

The publishers and I wish to express our thanks to those who have given advice in the making of this book. For Very Simple Arabic, we are especially indebted to Desmond Cosgove and Patrick de Courcy-Ireland. For *Simple Etiquette in Arabia*, we are especially grateful to Hussein Dabbagh, Frederick Sullivan, Paul Mahmood and Dr S. Darsh, former Imam of the London Mosque.

J.P.

PART I

Very Simple Arabic

Contents

At The Airport

Good Morning

Sa<u>baah</u> al-khair

(Greeting)

Sa<u>baah</u> an-noor

(Reply)

General Greeting

As-sa<u>laam</u> a<u>layku</u>m

(Greeting)

Peace be with you

Wa a<u>layku</u>m as-sa<u>laam</u>

(Reply)

And with you peace

or Hello

Mur<u>hu</u>ba

(Greeting)

Mur<u>hu</u>ba

(Reply)

Good Afternoon

and

Good Evening

Masaa al-<u>khair</u>

(Greeting)

Masaa an-<u>noor</u>

(Reply)

2

How are you?

Kayf haalak?*

(Greeting)

I am well

Al-humdoolillah bikhair

(Reply)

Thanks be to God

* 'Kayf haalik'

to a woman. The same reply

and you?

Wa inta?

(Greeting)

Al-humdoolillah

(Reply)

Goodbye

Maa as-sal<u>aa</u>ma

(Greeting)

Allah yisullmak

(Reply)

Good Night

Tisbah ala khair

(Greeting)

Wa inta min ahla

(Reply)

See you tomorrow

Ashoofak b**u**kra

Sharruftna

(lit . 'You have honoured me / us' – said by host)

*E*nglish is spoken in most airports but the following phrases may be useful:

I don't understand	Ana maa afham
Do you speak English?	Tatakullum Ingleezi?
I have this (to declare) only	Aindee haadha fuqut*
I have nothing (to declare)	Ma aindee shee
This is necessary for my work (e.g. samples)	Haadha dharooree li-amalee
Where is the toilet please?	Wayn al-hammaam minfudluk?
Where is the bank please?	Wayn al-bank minfudluk?
Where is my bag?	Wayn shantati?
Porter!	Ham<u>maal</u>!
This is mine	Haadha lee
There is one bag missing	Naaqis shanta
How much is that?	Kam?
How may kilometres is it to the town?	Kam keeloomitr lil balad?
Get me a taxi please	Utlub lee taxi minfudluk
I want to hire a car	Ureed asta'jir saiyaara
Where is the bus to the city?	Wayn al-bus lil madeena?
Where is the British Consulate	Wayn al-Cons*u*leeya al-Bareetaaneeya?

* You will frequently hear '*bass*' – the alternative word for 'only'

6

2

In A Taxi

Il al-<u>fu</u>nd<u>u</u>k Sheratoon minfudluk

To the Sheraton Hotel please

Na'am Seedee (or aiwa Seedee)

Yes Sir

Kam?

How much?

Khamsta'sher ree<u>yaal</u>

Fifteen riyals

La, katheer

No, that's a lot

Itna'shar ree<u>yaal</u>

Twelve riyals

Taiyyib!

Good!

Kam keeloomitr il al-Heeltoon?

How many kilometres to the Hilton?

Ashara, Seedee

Ten, Sir

If you wish to give directions

Ruh seeda, minfudluk

Go straight ahead, please

Il al-ye<u>saar</u> hina

To the left here

Il al-ya<u>meen</u>

To the right

Woqqof hi<u>naak</u> minfudluk

Stop there please

Bisir'a minfudluk

Faster please

Bib*u*t minfudluk

Slower please

Intadhar hina minfudluk

Wait here please

Aarja ba'd khamsa daqaa'iq

I will be back in five minutes

3

In An Hotel

As-sa<u>laam</u> a<u>layk</u>*u*m

(Greeting)

Peace be with you

Wa a<u>layk</u>*u*m as-salaam

(Reply)

And with you peace

Ismee Beeters*

My name is Peters

* There is no 'P' in Arabic

Aindee hajz

I have a reservation

or . . .

Ureed ghurfa minfudluk

I want a room please

Ureed ghurfa li shakhsain laha hammaam

I want a double room with bath

Fee mukayyif?

Is there air conditioning?

Kam al-eejaar li muddat yome?

How much is it (lit. *the 'rent'*) *per day?*

Eindak ghurfa arkhas min dhaalik?

Have you a room cheaper than that?

Ureed ashoof al-ghurfa minfudluk

I want to see the room please

La. Maa ahibha

No. I don't like it

Fee ghurfa ahsan?

Is there a better room?

Haadha taiyyib

This is fine

Meen?

Who?

Risaala, Seedee

A message, Sir

Lahdha minfudluk

A moment, please

Ta'aal!

Come in!

Illak Seedee

For you, Sir

*E*nglish is spoken in most hotels but the
following phrases may be useful:

What is the number of my room?	Aysh raqm ghurfatee?
My room number is . . .	Raqm ghurfatee . . .
Where is the bathroom?	Wayn al-hammaam?
This is broken	Haadha maksoor
This is my laundry	Haadha ghaseelee
When will it be ready?	Aymta haadir?
I want to leave this in the safe	Ureed atrak haadtha fil khazna
Is there a message for Mr Peters?	Fee risaala li-Saiyid Beeters?
Where is the telephone please?	Wayn at-telefoon minfudluk?
I want a telephone number	Ureed raqm at-telefoon
I want to send a telex message	Ureed arsil risaala bit-telex
I want to post a letter	Ureed arsil maktoob bil bareed
Have you got an English newspaper?	Aindak jareeda Ingleezeeya?
I want to change some travellers' cheques	Ureed tahweel sheekaat seeyaaheeya
I want a taxi please	Ureed taxi minfudluk
I want to hire a car with a driver	Ureed asta'jir saiyaara bi saa'iq
I want to hire a car without a driver	Ureed asta'jir saiyaara bidoon saa'iq
I am in a hurry	Ana musta'jil
The bill please	Al-hisaab minfudluk
What is this?	Aysh haadha?
There is a mistake here	Fee ghalat hina

4

Calling On An Arab

When calling on an Arab you must know the basic rules of etiquette[1]. A knowledge of the phrases below will give an excellent impression.

Welcome!

<u>Ah</u>lan wa <u>sah</u>lan!   <u>Ah</u>lan wa <u>sah</u>lan beek[2]

(Greeting)   (Reply)

[1] See Part II – *Simple Etiquette in Arabia*
[2] 'Beek**u**m' if replying to more than one person

Minfudluk astarreeh   Mash<u>koor</u>[1]

Please have a seat   *Thank you*

And following enquiries into each other's health . . .

Ta<u>fud</u>dal[2] sigaara   Aiwa

Please have a cigarette   *Yes*[3]

[1] Variant of 'sh*u*kraan'
[2] (lit. *be pleased to*)
[3] Do not say 'sh*u*kraan' (thank you) as in Arabia this often means 'No'.

Ta<u>fu</u>ddal qahwa?   Aiwa

Please have coffee?   *Yes*[1]

Ta<u>fu</u>ddal

Have this

Sh*u*kraan, bikuffee.

Thank you (i.e. *'no'*) *I have had sufficient*

[1] It would be impolite to refuse

21

Shukraan jazeelan

Thank you very much

Maa as-salaama

Goodbye

Baytee baytak

My house is your house

Shopping

Kam?	Ih<u>da</u>'shar deenaar
How much?	*Eleven dinars*

Shukraan,
a'teek khamsa

Thamaania, Seedee

Thank you,
I'll give you five*

Eight, Sir

Taiyyib, laakin ghaalee

La, rakhees

Good, but it is expensive

No, it is cheap

* 'Thank you' is often used to mean 'No' in Arabia

Haadha ad-dukkaan maftooh?

Is this shop open?

La, musakkar

No, it is closed

Tureed shee, Seedee?

You want something, Sir?

La, atafarraj fuqut

No, I'm just looking round

Shoof Seedee, shoof!

Look Sir, Look!

Shukraan, la

Thank you, no

In case you are troubled . . .

Baksheesh!

Baksheesh!

Imshee!

Go away!

Wayn 'maktab al-bareed' minfudluk?

Where is 'the post office' please?

The words below can be substituted between the inverted commas in this sentence . . .

Antique Shop	Dukkaan Anteeqaat
Bank	Baank
Bazaar	Sooq
Bookshop/stationer	Maktaba
Chemist	Saidalleeya
Clothes Shop	Dukkaan Malaabis
Dry Cleaner/laundry	Dukkaan Tandtheef Malaabis
Florist	Dukkaan Zuhoor
Jeweller	Dukkaan Jawaahir
Newsagent	Dukkaan Jaraa'id
Perfumery	Dukkaan Otoor
Photo Shop	Dukkaan Tasweer
Shoe Shop	Dukkaan Ahdheeya
Sports Shop	Dukkaan Reeyaadeeya
Tailor	Khayyaat
Tobacconist	Dukkaan Sigaayer
Travel Agent	Wakaalat Safar

Ureed ishteree 'qomees' minfudluk

Ta'aal!

Come!

I want to buy a shirt please

The words below can be substituted in this sentence . . .

Aspirin	Asbro
Book	Kitaab
Cigarettes	Sigaayer
Dictionary	Qaamoos
Envelopes	Dhuroof
Film	Film
Guide book of the city	Kitaab daleel al-madeena
Handkerchief	Mandeel
Ink	Hibr
Map of the town	Khaaritat al-balad
Magazine	Majalla
Newspaper	Jareeda
Notebook	Daftar
Pen	Qolum hibr
Pencil	Qolum rusaas
Pills	Huboob
Razor blades	Moos hallaaqa
Tissues	Mandeel woroq
Tobacco	Tombak
Toothbrush	Fursha lil-asnaan
Toothpaste	Ma'joon lil-asnaan
Towel	Manshafa
Writing paper	Woroq al-kitaaba

28

6

Travelling Around
and
Sightseeing

Mur<u>hu</u>ba

Hello

Mur<u>hu</u>ba

Hello

Wayn mahattat al-baas minfudluk?

Where is the bus station please?

Awwal sharri' alal-yesaar

The first street on the left

Ba'eed min hina?

Far from here?

La, qoreeb, khamsa daqaa'iq fuqut

No, it is close, five minutes only

M**u**mkin maashee?

Is it possible to walk?

Aiwa, arba'a meeyat mitr

Yes, four hundred metres

Wayn al-baas il Ar-Reeyaadh?

Where is the bus to Riyadh?

Haadhaak

That one

Il Ar-Reeyaadh minfudluk

To Riyadh please

Tafuddal

Be pleased to (get in)

Khabirnee aind al-wusool minfudluk

Inform me when we arrive please

Aiwa

Yes

Aymta tarooh?

When do you go?

Ba'ad ashara daqaa'iq

In ten minutes

Ureed azoor al-mat'haf minfudluk

I want to visit the museum please

Hinaak

Over there

Fee shee muhimm hina?

Is there anything of importance here?

Aiwa, ta'al

Yes, come

Taxi! ta'rif wayn maktab as-seeyaaha?

*Taxi! do you know where
the Tourist Office* is?*

The words below may be substituted in this sentence . . .

The Castle	Al-qal'a
The Church	Al-kaneesa
The Exhibition	Al-ma'rid
The Park	Al-bustaan
The Library	Al-maktaba
The Mosque	Al-masjid
The Old City	Al-madeena al-qodeema
The Ruins	Al-Aathaar
The University	Al-jaami'a
The Zoological Gardens	Al-hadeeqat al-haiyawaanaat

* Lit. (the) office (of) the tourism. See
explanation of 'Possession' on page 59

7

Leisure

A Pavement Cafe

Laymoon <u>baari</u>d minfudluk

A cold lemon drink please

Kam tureed?

How many do you want?

Ithnayn minfudluk

Two, please

Fee mat'am qoreeb min hina?

Is there a restaurant near here?

Minfudluk, nureed kabaab

Please, we would like kebab

The following words may be substituted in this sentence:

beer	beera*	*oranges*	burtuqaal
boiled	maslooq	*pepper*	filfil
bread	khubz	*potatoes*	bataata
butter	zibda	*rice*	ruz
cheese	jubna	*salad*	salaata
chicken	dajaaj	*salt*	milh
coffee	qahwa	*sandwich*	sand-weesh
eggs	baydh	*sauce/gravy*	salsa
fish	samak	*soup*	shoorba
fried/roasted	maqlee	*sugar*	sukkar
fruit	fawaakih	*tea*	shai
lemon	laymoon	*tomatoes*	tamaata
meat	lahm	*vegetables*	khudhra
melon	botteekh	*water*	moya
milk	haleeb	*wine*	nbeedh*

* In those countries where drinking alcohol is permitted

Aindak qahwa Nescafay?

Have you got Nescafe?

La, Turkeeya bass

No, Turkish coffee only

Al-hisaab minfudluk

The bill please

Ureed azoor maqha minfudluk

I want to visit a coffee-house please

The following words may be sustituted:

cinema	seenamaa
night club	malha layli
theatre	masrah

Fee cabaaray?

Is there a floor show?

The following words may be substituted:

belly-dancer	raaqisa sharqeeya
music	mooseeqa
dancing	raqs

Mumkin al'ab tennees hina?

Is it possible to play tennis here?

The following words may be substituted in this sentence:

golf	goolf
bowling	booling

Fee masbah hina?

Is there a swimming pool here?

Ma'loom!

Of course, certainly!

Ureed asbah fil bahr minfudluk

I want to swim in the sea, please.

Fee khatar hina?

Is there any danger here?

Mumkin sayd as-samak hina?

Is it possible to fish here?

8

Miscellaneous Phrases

Muta'assif! (or Aasif)

Sorry!

Ana ma araft

I didn't know

Shukraan   La shukraan ala waajib

Thank you   *Don't mention it*
                (lit. Don't thank me –
                it was my duty)

Inta lateef

You are kind

Maa laysh (or Maa y*u*khaalif)
Never mind

(Often accompanied by a shrug of the shoulders)

Ismahlee

Excuse me

Tatakullum Arabee?

Do you speak Arabic?

Bass qoleel

Only a little

Inta Amerikaanee?

Are you an American?

La, ana Ingleezee

No, I am English

Congratulations

Mabrook! Allah y*u*baarak feek

Lit. *'Blessed'* Lit. *'God bless you (too)'*

At Festival Time

Eed m*u*baarak!* Allah y*u*baarak feek

(Greeting) (Reply)

---

* Words used at the time of the two main religious festivals – See Part II – *Simple Etiquette in Arabia*

Exclamations!

Ya salaam!

Good Lord!

Wullah!

By God!

Mumtaz!

Excellent!

Al-<u>hum</u>doolillah

Thanks be to God

Other Useful Phrases

Ashoofak bukra

See you tomorrow

Inshaalah!*

If God wills!

A common reply acknowledging God's will over all things. Lit. In shaa'Allah – if (it is) God's will.

Fee hallaaq hina minfudluk?

Is there a barber here please?

Wayn fee tabeeb minfudluk?

Where is there a doctor please?

You may substitute the following in this sentence:

    dentist   tobeeb al-asnaan
    optician   ikhsa'i an-nadharaat

Eindee waj'a hina

I have a pain here

Haadha maksoor

This is broken

Finally you may find the following useful:

Aysh ism haadha minfudluk?

What is the name of this please?

Qul-lee murra thaaneeya

Say (lit. Tell me) it again

Utlub ash-shurta

Call the Police

At-toqs taiyyib al-yome

The weather is fine today

9
Numbers
and
Days of the Week

1	١	<u>waa</u>hid
2	٢	ith<u>nayn</u>
3	٣	thal<u>aa</u>tha
4	٤	<u>arb</u>a'a
5	٥	<u>kham</u>sa
6	٦	<u>sit</u>ta
7	٧	<u>sab</u>a'a
8	٨	tha<u>maa</u>nia
9	٩	<u>tis</u>'a
10	١٠	<u>ash</u>ara

11	١١	ih<u>da</u>'shar
12	١٢	<u>it</u>naa'shar
13	١٣	thalaa<u>tht</u>aashar
14	١٤	arba'<u>taa</u>'shar
15	١٥	khams<u>taa</u>'shar
16	١٦	si<u>tt</u>aa'shar
17	١٧	<u>saba</u>'tashar
18	١٨	thama<u>nta</u>'shar
19	١٩	<u>tis</u>'ataa'shar
20	٢٠	ishr<u>een</u>
30	٣٠	thl<u>aa</u>theen
40	٤٠	<u>ar</u>ba'een
50	٥٠	<u>kham</u>seen
60	٦٠	<u>sit</u>teen
70	٧٠	<u>saba</u>'een
80	٨٠	tham<u>aan</u>ee-een
90	٩٠	<u>tis</u>'aeen
100	١٠٠	meeya

Numbers after twenty are made up as follows:

    25 = <u>Kham</u>sa wa ish<u>reen</u>
    26 = <u>Sitt</u>a wa ish<u>reen</u>

There is no indefinite article (a/an) in Arabic and it is unnecessary to qualify a single object by using '<u>waa</u>hid' (one) e.g. '<u>wu</u>lud' means 'a' or 'one' boy

There is a special way of saying two of anything in Arabic. You add the ending 'ayn' to the noun

    '<u>wu</u>lud'   'wulud<u>ayn</u>'

This form is called the dual.

from 3 to 10 the accompanying noun is in the plural, but from eleven onwards it is in the singular, e.g.

> thala<u>aa</u>tha awlaad = *three boys*
> ish<u>reen</u> <u>wul</u>ud = *twenty boys*

Composite numbers are written from left to right, e.g. ١٩٧٨ = 1978

(Unlike Arabic script which is written from right to left)

Days of the Week

Sunday	Yome al-ahad
Monday	Yome al-ith<u>nayn</u>
Tuesday	Yome ath-thal<u>aa</u>tha
Wednesday	Yome al-<u>arb</u>a'a
Thursday	Yome al-<u>kham</u>ees
Friday	Yome al-<u>jum</u>a'a
Saturday	Yome as-sabt

SIMPLE GRAMMAR

The Arabic script looks complicated. In fact there are only a few more letters and sounds than in English and the rules of Grammar are, if anything, simpler.

There is no 'P' or 'V' in Arabic and an Arab will substitute 'B' and 'F' respectively, e.g. 'Peters' is pronounced 'Beeters' and 'Victor' is 'Fictor'.

Arabic script runs from right to left but figures are written from left to right*.

The definite article is 'al'. In front of words beginning with t th d dh s sh r z n and sometimes j the 'l' of the article is assimilated. So *al-shams* (the sun) becomes *ash-shams*.

Nouns in Arabic are either masculine or feminine in gender. Nouns referring only to females are obviously feminine. So are most nouns ending in 'a'. But otherwise there is often no clue to the correct gender which must be learnt.

As explained in Chapter 9, there are three 'numbers' in Arabic – singular, dual and plural. Plurals are not formed as in English. They are mostly variants of the singular and again are best memorised. You should note however that some masculine nouns form their plural simply by adding 'een' e.g.

Singular	*Plural*
Muslim (male)	Muslimeen

and that feminine nouns ending in 'a' form the plural by adding 'aat' e.g

Singular	*Plural*
Hukooma (Government)	Hukoomaat

* See page 61

Adjectives follow their noun. If the noun is definite then the adjective also carries the definite article.

Al-<u>wu</u>lud as-sagheer = *The small boy*

Normally they agree with the noun in gender and number. However, when the noun refers to plural 'things' or 'animals' then the adjective becomes feminine singular by adding the suffix 'a'. For example:

As-sanawaat al-akheer*a* = *The recent years*

The comparative of most adjectives takes the following forms:

> akbar – *greater*
> arkhas – *cheaper*
> akthar – *more*

Verbs in Arabic have only two tenses – one denoting completed action and the other, incompleted action. In simple terms this means a past tense and a present tense. The present tense is also used to cover the future. For example:

> katab means *he wrote* (past)
> yakt*u*b can mean *he is writing* (present)
> or *he will write* (future)

The verb 'to be' does not exist in the present tense. For example:

Al-<u>wu</u>lud sagheer means *The boy (is) small*

'*There is*' and '*there are*' are translated by 'fee' followed by the noun in the singular or plural. For example:

> Fee hallaaq hina? *Is there a barber here?*
> Fee booyoot hinnaak? *Are there houses over there?*

'*There was*' and '*there were*' are translated by 'kaan fee'.

57

Simple regular verbs in Arabic consist of a root of three consonants and when an Arab refers to a verb he uses the third person singular:

katab   *he wrote i.e. 'to write'* *

The past tense is formed by attaching suffixes to the root:

katabt	*I wrote*
katabt	*you* (masc) *wrote*
katabtee	*you* (fem) *wrote*
katab	*he wrote*
katabat	*she wrote*
katabna	*we wrote*
katabtoo	*you* (pl) *wrote*
kataboo	*they wrote*

Note: The subject pronoun is normally omitted when using a verb in Arabic e.g.

'katab kitaab' means '*he wrote a book*'.

The present/future tense is formed by adding a prefix (and sometimes a suffix as well) to the modified root and by changing its second vowel:

ak*tu*b	*I write*
tak*tu*b	*you* (masc) *write*
tak*tu*bee	*you* (fem) *write*
yak*tu*b	*he writes*
tak*tu*b	*she writes*
nak*tu*b	*we write*
tak*tu*boo	*you* (pl) *wrote*
yak*tu*boo	*they write*

The vowel change varies and must be learnt for each verb.

The 'imperative' is formed on the following pattern:

U**k**t*u*b! = *Write!*

* There is no infinitive in Arabic

The negative is formed by putting 'maa' in front of the verb:

> Maa katabt   *I did not write*

The imperative is negated by prefixing 'laa':

> Laa **u**kt**u**b!   *Don't write!*

Personal pronouns are as follows:

ana	*I*
inta	*you* (masc)
intee	*you* (fem)
hoowa	*he/it*
heeya	*she/it*
nehna	*we*
int**u**m	*you* (pl)
h**u**m	*they*

Possession is denoted by attaching suffixes to the noun:

ee	*my*
ak	*yours* (masc) *yours* (fem)
ik	*yours* (fem)
oh	*his*
ha	*hers*
na	*ours*
k**u**m	*yours* (pl)
h**u**m	*theirs*

e.g. baytak = *your house*

When a noun has a feminine ending 'a' then a 't' is put in front of the suffix:

> Saiyaaratee = *My car*

The object of the verb is also denoted by the use of the same suffix, with the exception that 'ee' becomes 'nee'.

> Darubnee = *He struck me*

'To have' is expressed in Arabic by adding the same suffixes to the word 'aind'. For example:

aindee   *I have*
aindak   *you have*

Possession otherwise has a special rule in Arabic. '*The house of the boy*' is not translated as such. In Arabic this would be

Bayt al-<u>wu</u>lud = *(The) house (of) the boy*

i.e. the definite article is dropped from the first word

Names are considered to be 'definite' so that '*Mohammed's house*' is written as

Bayt M*u*hammed

To ask a question use the same intonation of voice as in English

Aindak qahwa? = *Have you coffee?*

There is much more to Arabic grammar than this but it is hoped that these simplified rules will be a helpful introduction.

BASIC VOCABULARY

Plurals are shown in brackets

about	hawl	*barber*	hallaaq
above	foqe	*bazaar*	sooq
accident	haadith	*bathroom*	hammaam
	(hawaadith)	*beautiful*	jameel
across	aber	*because*	leeyan
adviser	mustashaar	*bed*	firaash
	(mustas-	*beer*	beera
	haareen)	*before*	qobl
after	ba'd	*behind*	wora
afternoon	ba'd adh-dhuhr	*belly dancer*	raaqisa
again	murra	*beneath*	taht
	thaaneeya	*beside*	jamb
against	did	*better*	ahsan
air conditioner	mukayyif	*between*	bayn
aircraft	taiyaara	*big*	kabeer
	(taiyaaraat)	*bill*	hisaab
airport	mataar	*bird*	tayr (tuyoor)
Algeria	Al-Jazaa'ir	*black*	aswad
all	kull	*blue*	azrak
also	aidan	*boat*	markab
always	daiman		(maraakib)
ambassador	safeer (sufaraa)	*boiled*	maslooq
America	Amreeka	*book*	kitaab (kutub)
and	wa	*bookshop*	maktaba
angry	za'laan	*bowling*	booling
animal	haiyawaan	*box*	sundook
	(haiyawaanaat)		(sanaadeek)
answer	jawaab	*boy*	wulud (awlaad)
antiques	anteeqaat	*brass*	nuhaas
apples	tuffaah	*bread*	khubz
April	Neesaan	*breakfast*	futoor
Arab	Arabee (Arab)	*bring me*	jeeblee
Arab Gulf	Al-Khaleej	*Britain*	Bireetaaneeya
	Al-Arabee	*broken*	maksoor
army	jaysh (juyoosh)	*brother*	akh (ikhwa)
assistant	muaawin	*brown*	asmar
	(muaawineen)	*brush*	fursha (furash)
at	aind	*bus*	baas (basaat)
attack	hujoom	*but*	walaakin
August	Aab	*butter*	zibda
		he buys	yashtaree
back	dhahr	*he bought*	ishtaraa
bad	battaal	*by..*	bi-..
bag	shanta		
baker	khabbaaz	*cake*	kaa'k
bananas	mowse	*Cairo*	Al-Qaahira
bank	baank	*camel*	jamal (jimaal)

camera	aalat at-tasweer/ cameera	cook	tabbakh
		correct	saheeh
		cost	qeema
capital city	aasima	country	bilaad (buldaan)
car	saiyaar (saiyaaraat)		
		crime	jareema (jaraa'im)
carpet	sajjaada		
he carried	hamal	cross	soleeb
he carries	yahmil	crowd	jumhoor (jamaahir)
castle	qal'a		
centre	markaz	cup	finjaan (fanaajeen)
certificate	shahaada		
chair	kursee (karaasee)	custom	aada (aadaat)
		Customs (Airport)	Jumruk
cheap	rakhees		
cheaper	arkhas		
cheese	jubna	Damascus	Dimashq
chemist shop	saidalleeya	dancing	raqs
chief	ra'ees	danger	khatar
chicken	dujaaja (dajaaj)	date	taareekh
		date (edible)	tamr (tumoor)
China	As-Seen	dawn	fajar
Christian	Maseehee (Masee-heeyeen)	day	yome (ayaam)
		December	Kaanoon Al Awwal
church	kaneesa	defence	difaa'
cigarette	sigaara (sigaayer)	delicious	ladheedh
		dentist	tobeeb al-asnaan
cinema	seenamaa		
circle	daa'ira	desert	baadia/sahraa
city	madeena (mudun)	deputy	wokeel (wukalaa)
clean	nodtheef	dictionary	qaamoos
clever	shaatir	difference between	farq bane
clock/hour	saa'a (saa'aat)		
clothing	libaas	difficult	saa'b
club	naadee	direction	jiha
coast	saahil	director	mudeer (mudara)
coffee	qahwa		
coffee-house	maqha	dirty	wosokh
cold	baarid	distance	musaafa
college	kulleeya	district	muntaqa (manaatiq)
colour	lone (alwaan)		
commerce/ trade	tijaara	division (parts)	qism (aqsaam)
		he did	'amil
complaint	shakwa	he is doing	ya'mal
concerning	bi-khusoos	doctor	tobeeb
Congratulations!	Mabrook!	dog	kalb (kilaab)
Consulate	Consuleeya	dollar	doolaar (doolaaraat)
contract	aqd (uqood)		

donkey	himaar	*exit*	makhraj
door	baab (abwaab)	*expense*	masroof
dress	libaas		(massaareef)
drink	mashroob	*expensive*	ghaalee
	(mashroobaat)	*experiment*	tajriba
driver	saa'iq		(tajaarib)
	(suwwaaq)	*expert (in)*	khabeer (bi)
dry	naashif	*explosion*	infijaar
during	khilaal	*exports*	saadiraat
dust	turaab	*external*	khaarijee
duty	waajib	*eye*	ain (uyoon)
	(waajibaat)		
		face	wajh
each of	kul min	*family*	aa'ila
early	bakeer	*far..from*	ba'eed..'an
earth	ard	*fare (taxi)*	ujra
east	sharq	*fat (adj)*	sameen
easy	sahal	*feast – at end*	Eid Al Fitr
he ate	akal	of Ramadan	
he eats	yaakul	*feast – at end*	Eid Al Adha
egg	bayda (bayd)	of the sacrifice	
Egypt	Misr	*February*	Shoobaat
electricity	kahraba	*festival*	Eid
embassy	sifaara	*few*	qoleel
employee	muwadhdhaf	*film*	film (aflaam)
	(muwad-	*finally*	akheeran
	hdhafeen)	*finger*	usbu' (asabi)
empty	faarrigh	*fire*	naar (fem)
end	nihaaya	*fish*	samak (asmak)
engineer	muhandis	*fishing*	sayd as-samak
	(muhandiseen)	*flag*	alam
English	Ingleezee	*earth/floor*	ardh
envelope	dharf (dhuroof)	*floor show*	cabaaray
equipment	jihaaz (ajhiza)	*it flew*	taar
(piece of)		*it flies*	yateer
equipment	udda (udad)	*flower*	zahr (zuhoor)
(military)		*food*	akl
especially	khusoosan	*foot*	qodom
essential	jowharee		(aqdaam)
evening	masaa	*for*	li
evening	sahra	*forbidden*	mamnoo'
entertainment		*foreign*	ajnabee
every	kull		(ajnaanib)
exactly	tamaaman	*he forgot*	nasee
for example	mathalan	*he forgets*	yansa
except	illa	*France*	Faransa
excellent	mumtaaz	*free*	hurr
exhibition	ma'rid	*French*	Fransaawee
it existed	wajad	*friend*	sodeeq
it exists	yoojad		(asdiqaa)

fried/roasted	maqlee	hard	saa'b
from	min	hat	qubba'a
frontier	hudood	head	raas
fruit	fawaakih	headcloth	kafeeyya
fuel	wuqood	headquarters	qeeyaada
full	malyaan	health	sahha
future	mustaqbal	heart	qolb
		heat	haraara
gallon	gaaloon	heavy	thaqeel
garment	thawb (theeyaab)	help	awn
		here	hina
gate	baab (abwaab)	high	aalee
general	aam	hire	eejaar
generous	kareem	he hired	ista'jar
Germany	Almaaneeya	he hires	yasta'jir
gift	hadeeya (hadaayaa)	holiday	utla
		honest	ameen
girl	bint (banaat)	horizontal	ufqee
he gave	aataa	horse	hisaan (husn)
he gives	yaatee	hot	haar
glad	farhaan	hotel	funduq (fanaadiq)
glass (drinking)	kubaaya	hour	saa'a (saa'aat)
he went	raah	house	bayt (buyuoot)
he goes	yarooh	how?	kayf?
he went in	dakhal	how many/ how much?	kam?
he goes in	yadkhul	hungry	jo'aan
he went out	kharaj	hurry (in a)	musta'jil
he goes out	yakhruj	hunting	sayd
goat	ma'z	husband	zawj (azwaj)
God	Allah		
gold	dhahab	ice	thalj
golf	goolf	identity card	huweeya
good	taiyyib	if	idha
government	Hukooma	ill	mareedh
green	akhdhar	immediately	haalan
group	jamaa'a	he imported	istawrad
guard	haras	he imports	yastawrid
guest	dhayf (dhuyoof)	imports	waaridaat
guide	daleel	important	muhim
guidebook	kitaab daleel	in	fee
Gulf	Khaleej	incident	haadith (hawaadith)
gun	madfa (madaafi)		
		he informed	khabbir
hair	sha'r	he informs	yukhbir
half	nus	India	Al-Hind
hand	yad (aydin)	information	khabar
handkerchief	mandeel	ink	hibr
happy	farhaan	inside	daakhil
harbour	meena		

international	duwalee	life	haiyaat
invitation	da'wa	light	noor
island	jazeera	like (adverb)	mithl
	(jazaa'ir)	he liked/loved	habb
Italy	Eetaaliya	he likes/loves	yahibb
		a little	qoleel
jacket	jaakeet	London	Lundun
		he looked	tafarraj
January	Kaanoon	around	
	Ath-Thani	he looks	yatafarraj
Jerusalem	Al-Quds	around	
Jew, Jewish	Yahoodee	love	hubb
Jews	Yahood	lunch	ghada
jewels	jawaahir		
Jordan	Al-Urdun	machine	makeena
job	wadheefa	mad	majnoon
journalist	sahaafee	magazine	majalla
	(sahaafeeyeen)	man	rajul (rijaal)
July	Tammooz	manager	mudeer
juice	aseer		(mudaraa)
June	Khuzayraan	many	katheer
		map	khaarita/
key	miftaah		khareeta
	(mafaateeh)	March	Aadhaar
kilometre	keelomitre	market	sooq
kind	lateef	married	mutazowwij
king	malik	May	Ayaar
kingdom	mamlaka	meat	lahm
knife	sikeen	Makkah (the	Makkah (Al
he knew	araf	Holy)	Mukarram)
he know	ya'rif	meeting	ijtimaa'
knowledge	ilm		(ijtimaa'aat)
Kuwait	Al-Koowayt	melon	botteekh
		merchant	taajir (tujjaar)
last (adj)	aakhir	message	risaala (rasaa'il)
late	Muta'akhkhir	metre	mitr (amtaar)
lately	Akheeran	middle	wost
law	qaanoon	Middle East	Ash-Sharq Al-
	(qawaaneen)		Owsat
lazy	kaslaan	military (adj)	askaree
leader	qaa'id	milk	haleeb
	(quwaad)	million	milyoon
Arab League	Al-Jaami'a Al-		(malaayeen)
	Arabeeya	minaret	minaara
Lebanon	Lubnaan	minister	wozeer (wuzaraa)
left	yesaar	ministry	wizaara
leg	rijl (arjul)	Ministry of:	Wizaaret . . .
lemon	laymoon	Agriculture	Az-Ziraa'a
letter	maktoob	Aviation	At-Taiyaaraan
library	maktaba	Commerce	At-Tijaara

65

Communi-	Al-Muwaasillat	north	shimaal
cations		notebook	daftar (dafaatir)
Education	At-Tarbeeya	November	Tishreen Ath-
Defence	Ad-Difaa		Thaanee
Development	Al-I'maar	number	raqm (arqaam)
Finance	Al-Maaleeya		
Health	As-Sahha		
Industry	As-Sinaa'a	October	Tishreen Al-
Interior	Ad-		Awwal
	Daakhileeya	office	maktab
Labour	Al-Amal		(makaatib)
Marine	Al-Bahreeya	oil (petroleum)	naft
Public Works	As-Ashghaal	oil (vegetable or	zayt
	(Al-Aamma)	lubricating)	
Transport	An-Naqleeyaat	old	qodeem
minute	daqeeqa	Oman	Umaan
	(daqaa'iq)	on	ala
mistake	ghalat	onions	bassal
modern	hadeeth	on the subject	bikhusoos
moment	lahdha	of . . .	
	(lahdhaat)	only	fuqut/bass
money	fuloos	open	maftooh
moon	qamr	opportunity	fursa
morning	sabaah	or	ow
Morocco	Al-Maghrib	oranges	burtuqaal
mosque	masjid	other	aakhar
most of	aghlab min		(fem)ukhra
Mr	Saiyid	outside	kharrij
mountain	jebal (jibaal)	over	ala/foqe
much	katheer		
Muscat	Musqat		
music	mooseeqa	pain	waj'a
Muslim	Muslim	Palestine	Filasteen
	(Muslimeen)	paper (pieces	woroqa
		of)	(awraaq)
name	ism (asmaa)	park	bustaan
navy	bahreeya	Parliament	Barlamaan
near (to)	qoreeb (min)	part (of)	juz (ajzaa)
necessary	dharooree	party	hufla
neighbour	jar (jeeraan)	political party	hizb (ahzaab)
never	abadan	passenger	raakib
new	jadeed		(rukkaab)
news	khabar	passport	jawaaz Safar
	(akhbaar)	past	maadee
newspaper	jareeda	the past	al-maadee
	(jaraa'id)	peace	silm
night	layl (layaali)	pen	qolum hibr
no	la	pencil	qolum rusaas
noise	sowt	people	naas
noon	dhuhr	(collectively)	

66

the (or a) people	ash-sha'b	*reason*	sabab (asbaab)
pepper	filfil	*recent*	akheer
period	mudda	*red*	ahmar
permission/ permit	rukhsa	*Red Sea*	Al-Bahr Al-Ahmar
person	shakhs (ashkhaas)	*religion*	deen
		rent	eejaar
petrol	benzeen	*reply*	jawaab (ajwiba)
photograph	soora (suwar)	*repair*	tasleeh
pills	huboob	*report (of committee)*	taqreer (taqaareer)
place	mahal	*reservation*	hajz
please	minfudluk	*he reserved*	hajaz
police	shurta	*he reserves*	yahjaz
policeman	shurtee	*responsible (for)*	mas'ool (an)
police station	mahattat ash-shurta	*responsibility*	mas'ooleeya
poor	faqeer	*rest (ease)*	raaha
pork	lahm khanzeer	*the rest of*	al-baaqee min
porter	hammaal	*restaurant*	mat'am
possible	mumkin	*result (of)*	nateeja (min) nataa'ij
post	bareed		
post office	maktab al-bareed	*he returned*	raja'a
		he returns	yija'a
potatoes	bataata	*rice*	ruz
present (adj)	haalee	*rich*	ghanee
present (gift)	hadeeya (hadaayaa)	*rifle*	bunduqeeya (banaadiq)
Prime Minister	Ra'ees Al-Wuzara	*right (opposite of left)*	yameen
press (noun)	sahaafa	*river*	nahr
press (adj)	suhufee	*Riyadh*	Ar-Reeyaadh
principal (main)	raeesee	*room*	ghurfa (ghuraf)
problem	mushkila (mashaakil)	*round (circular)*	mudawwar
prohibited	mamnoo'	*ruins*	aathaar
public (ad)	umoomee	*ruler*	haakim
		roasted/fried	maqlee
qualification	salaaheeya (salaaheeyaat)	*Russia*	Rooseeya
queen	malika	*sad*	hazeen
question	su'aal (as'ila)	*safe (adj)*	saalim
quickly	bisir'a	*safe (n)*	khazna
quiet	haadee	*safety*	salaama
the Quran (the Holy)	Al-Quraan (Al-Kareem)	*salad*	salaata
		salt	milh
Rabat	Ar-Rabaat	*Sana'a*	Sana'a
rain	matar	*sand*	raml
razor blades	moos hallaaka	*sandwich*	sandweesh
ready	haadir	*sauce/gravy*	salsa

Saudi Arabia	Al-Mamlaka	stairs	daraj
	Al-Arabeeya	stamp	taabi'
	As-Sowdeeya	(postage)	(tawaabi'a)
he said	qaal	star (lit and	najm (nujoom)
he says	yaqool	met)	
school	madrassa	station	mahatta
	(madaaris)	step	daraja
sea	bahr	stomach	botn
seat (chair)	kursee	stone	hajar (ahjaar)
	(karaasee)	street	sharri'a
secret (noun)	sirr (asraar)	strong	qowee
secret (adj)	sirree	student	taalib (tullaab)
secretary	sikriteer	Sudan	As-Soodaan
	sikriteera (fem)	sugar	sukkar
he saw	shaaf	summer	sayf
he sees	yashoof	sun	shams
September	Aylool	sweet	hiloo
servant	khaadim	he swam	sabah
	(khuddaam)	he swims	yasbah
service	khidma	swimming pool	masbah
at your service	fee khidmatak	Syria	Sooreeya
Sharjah	Ash-Sharja		
sheep (coll)	ghanam	table	taawula
Sheikh	Shaykh	tailor	khayyaat
shirt	qomees	he talked	takullum
shoes	ahdheeya	he talks	yatakullum
shop	dukkaan	target	hadaf (ahdaaf)
	(dakaakeen)	tax	dareeba
shore	shatt		(daraa-ib)
short	qoseer	tea	shai
shut	musakkar	technical (adj)	fannee
silver	fidhdha	technique	fann (Funoon)
simple	boseet	telegram	telegraaf
since (time)	mundh	telephone	telefoon
slow (adj)	butee	temperature	darajat al-
small	sagheer		haraara
Smoking	Mamnoo' At-	tennis	tenees
Prohibited	Tadkheen	tent	khayma
soldier	askaree (askar)		(khuyoom)
some of	ba'd Min	there is/are	fee
sometimes	ihyaanan	there was/were	kaan fee
soon (after a	ba'd kaleel	that	dhaalik
little)		theatre	masrah
soup	shoorba	there	hinaak
he spoke	takullum	thing	shee (ashyaa)
he speaks	yatakallum	thirsty	atshaan
specialist	ikhsaa'ee	this	haadha
spectacles	nadhaaraat	thousand	elf (aalaaf)
sport	reeyaadha	time	murra (murraat)
square	murubb'a	(occasional)	

68

time (period)	woqt (awqaat)	*he waited*	intadhar
tired	taa'baan	*he waits*	yantadhir
to	ila	*he walked*	mashaa
tobacco	tombak	*he walks*	yimshee
today	al-yome	*he wants*	yureed
toilet	hammaam	*water*	moya or maa
tomato	tamaata	*weak*	da'eef
tomorrow	bukra	*weapon*	silaah (asliha)
toothbrush	fursha lil-asnaan	*weather*	toqs
toothpaste	ma'joon lil-asnaan	*weight*	wazn
tourism	seeyaaha	*west*	gharb
tourist	saa'ih (suyyaah)	*what?*	aysh?
towel	manshafa (manaashif)	*when?*	aymta/matta?
town	balad	*where?*	wayn?
tree	shajara (ashjaar)	*which?*	ay?
tribe	qobeela (qabaa'il)	*while*	baynamaa
Tripoli	Taraabulus	*white*	abyad
trousers	bantaloon	*who?*	meen?
true (correct)	saheeh	*whole*	kul
truth	haqq	*why?*	laysh?
Tunisia	Toonis	*wind*	howa
Turkey	Turkeeya	*window*	shubbaak (shabaabeek)
type (mark)	tiraaz	*wine*	nbeedh
under	taht	*winter*	shita
he understands	fahim	*with*	ma
he understands	yafham	*without*	bidoon
university	jaami'a	*wireless*	la silkee
until	hatta	*woman*	hurma (hareem)
up	foqe	*word*	kalima (kalimaat)
useful	mufeed	*work*	shogl or amal
usual	aadi	*world*	aalam
usually	aadatan	*he wrote*	katab
valid	jayyid	*he writes*	yaktub
valley	waadee	*writing paper*	woroq al-kitaaba
value	qeema	*wrong (n)*	ghalat (aghlaat)
valuable	thameen	*wrong (adj)*	ghaltaan
vegetables	khudra	*yellow*	asfar
vertical	amoodee	*Yemen*	Al-Yaman
very	jiddan	*yes*	aiwa or na'am
village	qoriya (quraa)	*yesterday*	ams
he visited	zaar	*young small*	sagheer
he visits	yazoor	*zero*	sifar
		zoological gardens	hadeeqat al-haiyawaanaat

69

PART II

Simple Etiquette in Arabia

Contents

Some Useful Facts

Most Arabs are Muslims (it is also spelt Moslem). Their religion, Islam, was revealed to the Prophet Muhammad between 610 and 632 A.D.

The holy book is called the Quran, and is the foundation and primary source of doctrine in Islam. Fundamental to the believer is the fact that the Quran is the infallible word of God. It contains among other things a comprehensive code of conduct transforming human experience and knowledge into an order reflecting all aspects of life.

The public place of worship is the Mosque. . .

. . . which is attended mainly by men. Women either pray at home or use the special place allotted in most large Mosques. The call to prayer is chanted by the *Muezzin* from the Minaret.

On entering the Mosque and before praying the Muslim removes his shoes and washes his hands, face and feet. Prayer is led by the *Imam*.

Friday is the holy day of the week, although a Muslim must pray five times every day at:

Dawn
Noon
Afternoon
Sunset
Evening

Daily prayers do not have to be said in a Mosque. Muslims may pray wherever they happen to be at the time of prayer. This may be in an office or beside a road; don't be surprised, therefore, when you first see it. In Arabia it is a common everyday sight.

A Muslim, when he prays, always faces in the direction of the holy city of Makkah.

Arabic is the language of the Holy Quran. The script, written from right to left, has an alphabet of consonants. It is by no means easy to learn although the rudiments of the spoken language can be quickly mastered if you get down to it.

The pleasantries are included in subsequent chapters and if the foreigner takes the trouble to learn them he can be sure of an enthusiastic reception. In the author's experience, one is always given greater credit than is justified by one's efforts.

Women in many Arab countries wear a black cloak and may also be veiled (in purdah). In other Arab countries however, women dress in the European fashion. In any case, women are viewed in a special way in Arabia. One might for example, enquire after the health of the family of an Arab but not specifically of his wife.

The thing most likely to impress you about the Arab is his hospitality . . .

Baytee Baytak

My house is your house

. . . but his whole way of life, stemming as it does from his ancient heritage as well as from his environment may well catch your imagination.

2

On Meeting An Arab

Always shake hands. When they greet each other after a long absence it is customary for Arabs to kiss symbolically on each cheek. An Arab may also keep hold of your hand while he is talking to you after shaking hands. This is a normal custom in Arabia and is a mark of friendship.

The most common greetings are as follows:

Greeting   Reply

Greeting   Reply

Good Evening

Greeting   Reply

Hello

Greeting   Reply

81

Al-**humdoolillah** means that you are well (literally *'thanks be to God'*) and it is customary to always give this reply even if you are at death's door. (In saying this the Muslim is acknowledging God's will.)

forms of address are important. An Arab is called **Saiyid** (Mr) followed by the first of his given names, and when on familiar terms by the first of his given names only. A ruling Sheikh is *'Your Highness'* initially and thereafter *'Sir'*. Other Sheikhs are *'Your Excellency'* as are Government Ministers. When calling an Arab it is polite to prefix his name with **'Ya'**.

The two main variations for *'Goodbye'* are:

you may also hear **Allah Yisullmak** and **Salaamak-allah** used in reply.

3
You Pay A Call

After shaking hands and exchanging greetings the person on whom you call will ask you to sit down . . .

Your host will indicate a seat. The most important visitor usually sits on his host's right hand in the closest seat.

Don't be surprised if someone occupying that position gets up to make way for you. It means you are considered more important . . . for the moment anyway.

Don't sit in such a way that the sole of your foot is presented to another person. This used to mean, and still does in some places. that you are intentionally insulting that person (since the sole of the foot is unclean).

What happens next depends on your host. He may or may not follow the custom of consuming refreshments before discussing the purpose of your visit. His manner and general appearance will usually tell you what type of person he is. It is increasingly common in business circles to dispense with the formalities.

If, however, your host abides by the old customs there then follows a period either of silence or of general enquiries after each other's health. This lasts until a servant enters with tea or coffee.

Take the cup in the right hand. The right hand only is used when drinking, eating and offering cigarettes.

Drink as many cups as you like but not a lot more than your host or others present. It is customary, however, to drink more than one cup of coffee or milk-less tea or you risk offending your host. Turkish coffee should be sipped until an inch of the liquid remains in the cup or you may end up swallowing the thick coffee grounds.

The signal that you use to show you have had enough to drink is a quick twist of the empty cup as you hand it back.

The time is now opportune to mention the subject of your visit.

You may, as a businessman, have been ushered into a room and found other businessmen present. In this case announce yourself, sit down, drink any refreshment offered and wait to be asked your business. When asked, give enough information to interest your potential client so that he will consider granting you an exclusive interview later when you will be able to set out your terms in detail.

Do not admire anything belonging to your host. By custom he would be honour bound to make you a gift of it! Even if you succeed in refusing, it may take a long time.

It is inadvisable to work to a tight schedule in Arabia. Be on time for an appointment, but be prepared for it to be delayed (you may be kept waiting for several hours) or even postponed. This is not inefficiency but simply the result of a different way of life lived at a different pace. You will find, for example, that most Arabs keep *'open office'*, i.e. other people are free to enter at any time.

If you hand a gift to an Arab friend do not be surprised if he does not open it or even thank you for it. This is the normal custom in Arabia although it is difficult for Europeans to understand. He will also frequently start to refuse the gift, indicating that you should not have taken the trouble. But you should insist the gift be accepted.

Remembering Arab names is difficult but most Arabs have printed cards. It will help to have your own card printed in Arabic as well as English.

finally, never call at Siesta time . . .

4

A Hufla

Hufla is the Arabic word for party. You may be fortunate enough to receive an invitation. In which case. . .

your host would be most impressed to receive a written reply in Arabic if that is appropriate. An Arab friend might write it for you.

The time of your arrival will vary depending on the type and circumstances of the party and who the host is. It is sometimes correct to arrive exactly on time and at others to delay for five or so minutes or even longer. It is best to seek advice . . .

eating still sometimes takes place at floor level. Again avoid presenting the soles of your feet to anyone. Use only your right hand . . .

I t is customary to take your leave soon after you have drunk the coffee . . .

SUPER BLOKE

Y ou may also wish to entertain. Ideally, issue a written invitation in Arabic. Any local printer will help you. Do not attempt to mimic all the Arab customs. English food is quite acceptable except that the Muslim is forbidden by the laws of his religion to eat pork or drink alcohol.

When an Arab has visited you he may later make a small gift in thanks. You should reciprocate when next you are his guest.

———

5

Eids

The Arabic word for festival is **Eid.** There are a number of festivals each year but you need only concern yourself with the two most important . . .

EID AL-ADHA and EID AL-FITR

The exact day and month of any festival varies every year because the Muslim calendar (Hejira) is based on a lunar month cycle, which also means that the exact day of a given festival will differ from country to country.

Id Al Adha is the biggest festival and is celebrated at the same time as the pilgrimage to Makkah. An important feature of the pilgrimage is the circumambulation of the Kaaba which holds the 'black stone' sacred to all Muslims.

Id Al Fitr takes place at the end of the fast of Ramadan.

Ramadan lasts for a full lunar month. All Muslims are required to abstain from food, drink and tobacco and all other pleasurable pursuits between sunrise and sunset.

Naturally you should show consideration and not eat, drink or smoke in the presence of a Muslim during daylight hours. In any case, you will probably find it is a punishable offence to do so in some Arab countries. A Western woman should, in addition, dress soberly, i.e., she should not wear a short skirt.

Ramadan ends with a feast.

O n the occasion of both, the **Eid Al Adha** and the **Eid Al Fitr** greetings cards are sent (to arrive a day or two in advance) and often you will receive a card of thanks in reply. The greetings card which you should send will look like this:-

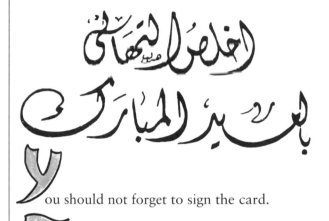

اخلص التهانى
بالعيد المبارك

Y ou should not forget to sign the card.

T he card you may receive in reply will look like this:-

أشكركم على تهانيكم بالعيد السعيد
وكل عام وانتم بخير

When you meet an Arab on the day of an **Eid** or in the days closely following it you would shake hands and use a special greeting:-

Greeting   Reply

On the occasion of both **Eids** it is the custom for important persons to hold audience in their palaces or home. You should enter the house, greet them, take coffee and leave after a suitable interval.

Arab families will visit each other at **Eid** time and any visiting foreigner will be equally as welcome during this period.

You may also give a small present to the children of an Arab family if you do visit one.

ONE AT A TIME LADS!

Miscellaneous Points

The first problem you face in Arabia may be the heat. It can make people who are not used to it short tempered.

The law concerning alcohol is strictly enforced in some Arab countries where the possession of even a small quantity is a punishable offence.

*Y*ou may also find a ban on the 'Playboy' type of magazine. Advice on these matters can easily be obtained – say from your airline before departure.

*T*axis in Arabia seldom have meters. It is wise for a newcomer to agree the fare in advance of the journey and so avoid any surprises. Tipping is customary in some Arab countries but not in the Gulf region. Tipping of porters is universal. Tipping in hotels and restaurants follows Western practice, i.e. tip if there is no service charge.

*I*t is often difficult for a Westerner to understand that prices in an Arab market (**sooq**) are flexible. Bargaining is part of the way of life. There are of course plenty of other shops where prices are fixed but this will be obvious to you.

In general conversation with an Arab, at least on first acquaintance, avoid talking about religion, women and the politics of the Middle East.

You will discover that the Arab sense of humour is remarkably like our own, and jokes generally are appreciated.

Don't be surprised when offering something to an Arab – say a cigarette – if he says 'thank you' but means by that phrase that he refuses. This way of saying 'no' is customary in Arabia.

A remarkable fact about Arabic is the absence of the equivalent of the European swear-word.

To an Arab a dog is unclean and he will not touch one, except perhaps the Saluki – the Arabian gazelle hound. If you should see small boys throwing stones at a dog it is not solely a question of cruelty.

The Arab uses his hands as a means of expression as much as a Frenchman does. Some of the most common gestures are . . . . . . putting the tips of the fingers and thumb together and moving the hand up and down to mean *Patience! Patience*!

. . . pulling the point of one's chin to mean . . .

. . .*'Shame!'*

. . . and putting the fingers together and pointing downwards when beckoning someone . . .

. . . do not beckon with one finger in the normal way as this has an offensive connotation in Arabia.

Sooner or later you will come across a particular variation of the customary handshake. If his hands are dirty, an Arab will offer you his right wrist which you should shake in the normal way.

Great care should be taken when producing a document or advertisement in Arabic. It is easy for a translator to render an English phrase into Arabic and for the result to be meaningless or even offensive.

Finally, here are five very common words, not previously mentioned, which you may find useful:-

Please

Thank you

(there are also other words)

Be pleased to

(when offering a seat, cigarette etc)

If God wills

Sorry

Glossary

Ahlan wa sahlan	Welcome and reply to hello
Ahlan wa sahlan beekum	Reply to Ahlan wa sahlan
Al-humdoolillah	Reply to 'How are you?' (Thanks be to God)
Allah yubaarak feek	Reply to Eid mubaarak
Allah yisallmak	Reply to Maa-as-salaama
As-salaam alaykum	General greeting (Peace be upon you)
Ayaamak Saayeeda	Reply to Eid mubaarak
Baytee baytak	My house is your house
Eid	Festival
Eid Al Adha	Festival at the time of the Pilgrimage
Eid Al Fitr	Festival at the end of Ramadan
Eid Mubaarak	Greeting at Eid Time (A Happy Eid)
Fi-amaan-illah	Goodbye
Ka'aba	Black stone in the Great Mosque in Makkah

Kayf haalak?	How are you?
Hufla	Party
In shaa'Allah	If God wills
Masaa al-khair	Good evening
Masaa an-noor	Reply to good evening
Ma-as-salaama	Goodbye
Murahuba	Hello
Minaret	Mosque tower
Minfudluk	Please
Muezzin	Caller to Prayer
Ramadan	Month of the Fast
Sabah al khair	Good Morning
Sabah an-noor	Reply to good morning
Salaamakallah	Reply to Ma-As-Salaama
Shukraan	Thank-you (plus variations)
Sooq	Market
Tafuddal	Please sit down (be pleased to)
Wa-alaykum as-salaam	Reply to as-salaam alaykum
Ya Ahmed	Polite form of address (Oh Ahmed)

109

NOTES